Made in United States
North Haven, CT
14 January 2024

47452051R00070